Learn2Draw

Learn2Draw

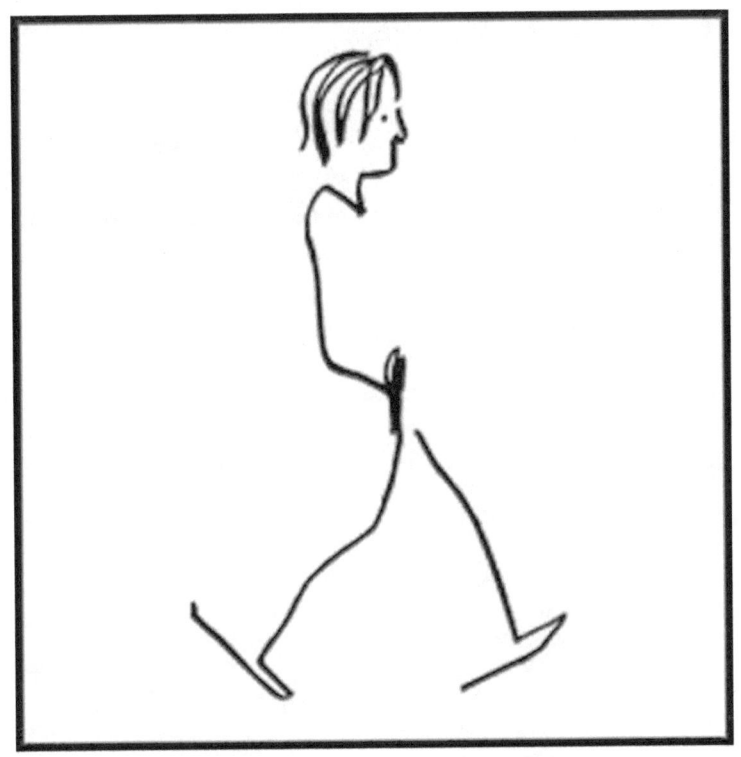

Wagner Anarca "Papis"

ISBN: Softcover   978-1-4836-0703-0
               Ebook   978-1-4836-0704-7

This book was printed in the United States of America.

Rev. date: 04/09/2013

To order additional copies of this book, contact:
Xlibris Corporation
1-888-795-4274
www.Xlibris.com
Orders@Xlibris.com
129601

INTRODUCTION

This book is an answer to the entire people that ask me about how to do drawings.

I like to read and watch everything that is coming to me about drawings, art, music, dance and poetry . . .

So my advice is: "Keep on drawing and drawing . . ."
"Keep your Sketchbook close than your cell phone"

A lot of fun sketching, scribbling, rendering, rough out, mark, shade, delineate, draft, crayon, caricature, limn, express it, etch, design, dropping a line, trace or doodle!!!!!!

Please, Have a Fun!!!!

LEARN2DRAW

LEARN2DRAW

LEARN2DRAW

LEARN2DRAW

LEARN2DRAW

LEARN2DRAW

LEARN2DRAW

LEARN2DRAW

LEARN2DRAW

LEARN2DRAW

LEARN2DRAW

LEARN2DRAW

LEARN2DRAW

LEARN2DRAW

LEARN2DRAW

LEARN2DRAW

LEARN2DRAW

LEARN2DRAW

LEARN2DRAW

LEARN2DRAW

LEARN2DRAW

LEARN2DRAW

LEARN2DRAW

LEARN2DRAW

LEARN2DRAW

LEARN2DRAW

LEARN2DRAW

LEARN2DRAW

LEARN2DRAW

LEARN2DRAW

LEARN2DRAW

LEARN2DRAW

LEARN2DRAW

LEARN2DRAW

LEARN2DRAW

LEARN2DRAW

LEARN2DRAW

LEARN2DRAW

LEARN2DRAW

LEARN2DRAW

LEARN2DRAW

LEARN2DRAW

LEARN2DRAW

LEARN2DRAW

LEARN2DRAW

LEARN2DRAW

LEARN2DRAW

LEARN2DRAW

LEARN2DRAW

LEARN2DRAW

LEARN2DRAW

LEARN2DRAW

LEARN2DRAW

LEARN2DRAW

LEARN2DRAW

LEARN2DRAW

LEARN2DRAW

LEARN2DRAW

LEARN2DRAW

LEARN2DRAW

LEARN2DRAW

LEARN2DRAW

LEARN2DRAW

LEARN2DRAW

LEARN2DRAW

LEARN2DRAW

LEARN2DRAW

LEARN2DRAW

LEARN2DRAW

LEARN2DRAW

LEARN2DRAW

LEARN2DRAW

LEARN2DRAW

LEARN2DRAW